Alternative Fuels and Energy Conservation

Alternative Fuels and Energy Conservation

SPECIAL SECRET RESOURCE!

Using Alternative Fuel - Doing Your Bit To Save The Environment!

Are You Aware Of The Damage Inflicted By The Fuel You Use For Your Vehicle? Are You Responsible Enough To Save The Environment From The Atrocities Of Man? Looking For An Alternative Source Of Fuel, But Not Sure Where To Even Start...?

Finally! Discover Some Of The Top Secrets That Gives You Premium Tips On Using Environmentally Friendly Fuel...! Learn Some Insider Tips To Increase Mileage, Save Money, Save The Environment, And Save A Trip Down To The Fuel Station...!

AVAILABLE ONLY FOR A VERY LIMITED TIME!

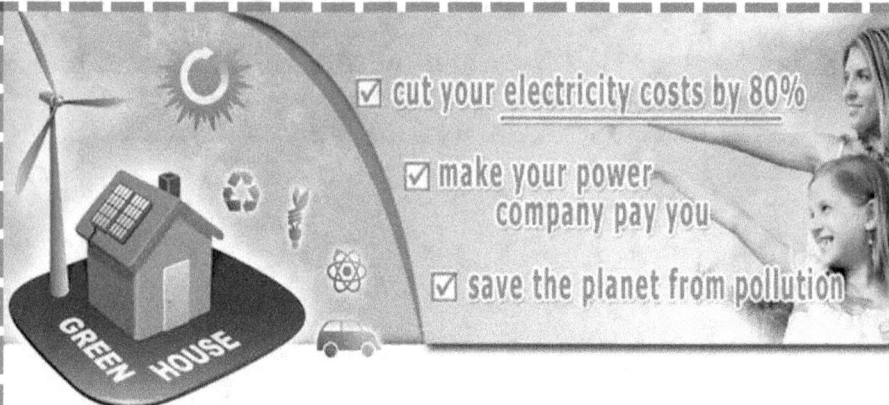

Home Made Power Plant

Discover How To Pay Only $3 For Electricity This Month... Next Month... Forever...

Discover The Naked Truth about Alternative Electricity!

 Save hundreds of dollars (even thousands) in electricity bill each month without lifting a finger.

 Earn a "fat" check every month from the power company for the extra electricity you produce.

 Extremely easy & cheap to build your own solar & wind generators (Approx. $200 investment and it will last a lifetime)

 Fully illustrated manual, and it is explained in plain English so even the least mechanically inclined person can understand and implement the ideas.

 Have a significant role in saving the planet because you'll be one of the pioneers who will help eradicate the huge deposits of CO2 killing our planet.

CLICK HERE Claim Your Copy "HomeMadePowerPlant"

Alternative Fuels and Energy Conservation

Contents

- What Are Alternative Fuels 9
- Why Are Gas Prices So High 11
- Alternative Fuel Vehicles 13
- Gasoline And Oil 15
- Environmental Damage 17
- Global Warming 19
- Alternative Fuel According To The Numbers 21
- Energy Conservation Throughout the Home 23
- Energy Conservation Through Your Piping 24
- Energy Conservation With Your Furnace 25
- Energy Conservation Outdoors 26
- Energy Conservation Tips To Get Started 27
- Electric Car Conversions 28
- Direct Methanol Fuel Cell 30
- Fuel Cells For Small Household Appliances 32
- Alternative Fuel Vehicles 34
- Alternative Fuel History 36
- Alternative Fuel Hummer 38
- Biodiesel Isn't The Only Game In Town 39
- Alternative Hydrogen Fuel Made On Site 40
- Types Of Alternative Fuels 42
- Alternative Energy For The Home 44
- Heating Water Using Solar Power 46
- Electric Car Facts 48
- New Electric Car Batteries- Every Car Freak's Dream Battery! 50
- E85 Ethanol Alternative Fuel 52
- Ethanol Fuel Varieties And Vehicles That Run On Them! 54
- Government Grants For Alternative Fuel 55
- Energy Conservation: Why It's So Important 57
- Energy Conservation Tips 58
- Energy Conservation: Save Gas 59
- Energy Conservation: Check Your Windows 60
- Energy Conservation: Alternative Energy Sources 62
- Energy Conservation: Small Things Add Up 63

Energy Conservation: Conserve By Using Your Thermostat 64
Energy Conservation: Consider Your Lighting 65
Energy Conservation In Decorating Your Home 66
Energy Conservation And The Fireplace 67

What Are Alternative Fuels

In the simplest form, an alternative fuel is one that is not produced by using crude oil. They are simply fuels that replace conventional gasoline as a means of powering vehicles. Alternative fuels have desirable energy efficiency and pollution reduction features. The 1990 Clean Air Act encourages development and sale of alternative fuels.

More specifically, the Energy Policy Act (EP Act) of 1993 gave a more in-depth definition of what they consider to be alternative fuels. The United States Department of Energy recognizes the following as alternative fuels:

- Mixtures containing 85% or more by volume of alcohol fuel, including methanol and denatured ethanol

- Natural gas (compressed or liquefied)

- Liquefied petroleum gas (propane)

- Hydrogen

- Coal-derived liquid fuels

- Fuels derived from biological materials

- Electricity (including electricity from solar energy)

- 100% Biodiesel (B100)

Pure biodiesel (B100) is considered an alternative fuel under EP Act. Lower-level biodiesel blends are not considered alternative fuels, but covered fleets can earn one EP Act credit for every 450 gallons of B100 purchased for use in blends of 20% biodiesel or higher.

Energy Conservation And Alternative Fuel

Through the Alternative Fuel Petition Program, third parties can petition the Department of Energy to add alternative fuels to the above list. People are always on the lookout for new ways to combat rising fuel prices and develop fuels that are not only good for the environment, but for the consumer's checkbook as well.

Basically, alternative fuels include methane, propane, ethanol, and compressed gas among others. We'll examine some of these a little later in the book, but alternative fuels don't fall into one compact category other than the one that defines them as an option over gasoline.

It's kind of exciting to think about the fact that we can now power our vehicles using things like vegetable oil, animal fats, and even wood! It brings to mind the movie "Back to the Future" where Doc would power his DeLorean time machine using garbage as fuel!

Why Are Gas Prices So High

There are three main grades of gasoline: regular, mid-grade, and premium. Each grade has a different octane level. Price levels vary by grade, but the price differential between grades is generally constant.

The cost to produce and deliver gasoline to consumers includes the cost of crude oil to refiners, refinery processing costs, marketing and distribution costs, and finally the retail station costs and taxes. The prices paid by consumers at the pump reflect these costs, as well as the profits (and sometimes losses) of refiners, marketers, distributors, and retail station owners.

In 2005 the price of crude oil averaged $50.23 per barrel, and crude oil accounted for about 53 percent of the cost of a gallon of regular grade gasoline. In comparison, the average price for crude oil in 2004 was $36.98 per barrel, and it composed 47 percent of the cost of a gallon of regular gasoline. The share of the retail price of regular grade gasoline that crude oil costs represent varies somewhat over time and among regions.

Federal, State, and local taxes are a large component of the retail price of gasoline. Taxes (not including county and local taxes) account for approximately 19 percent of the cost of a gallon of gasoline. Within this national average, Federal excise taxes are 18.4 cents per gallon and State excise taxes average about 21 cents per gallon. Also, eleven States levy additional State sales and other taxes, some of which are applied to the Federal and State excise taxes.

Additional local county and city taxes can have a significant impact on the price of gasoline. Refining costs and profits comprise about 19 percent of the retail price of gasoline. This component varies from region to region due to the different formulations required in different parts of the country.

Distribution, marketing and retail dealer costs and profits combined make up 9 percent of the cost of a gallon of gasoline. From the refinery, most gasoline is shipped first by pipeline to terminals near consuming areas, and then loaded into trucks for delivery to individual stations.

Energy Conservation And Alternative Fuel

Some retail outlets are owned and operated by refiners, while others are independent businesses that purchase gasoline for resale to the public. The price on the pump reflects both the retailer's purchase cost for the product and the other costs of operating the service station. It also reflects local market conditions and factors, such as the desirability of the location and the marketing strategy of the owner.

Because gasoline is made of crude oil, the biggest reason for the fluctuation in gas prices has to be the price of that crude oil. Essentially, crude oil prices are determined by supply and demand. However, world events can certainly affect the price of crude oil. The price on a barrel of oil rose sharply during the following world events:

- The Arab oil embargo in 1973
- The Iranian revolution in 1978
- The Iran/Iraq War in 1980
- The Persian Gulf Conflict in 1990
- The Iraq War currently being fought today

The turmoil occurring in these countries during these difficult times certainly affected production of oil and thus affected oil prices as well.

Believe it or not, even environmental and weather problems can affect gas prices. When Hurricane Katrina hit in 2005, some crucial oil refineries located in the region were devastated. That meant that oil had to be refined elsewhere and then transported. This increased fuel costs with the distance involved during this process.

Alternative Fuel Vehicles

There are two types of alternative fuel vehicles – those that are originally designed to run on these new fuels and those that have been converted to run on alternative fuels. Car companies will also make hybrid vehicles that can run on either gasoline or other fuels. Many people call these cars "green vehicles" because of their positive effect on the environment.

Since the trend is toward producing and buying environmentally friendly vehicles, nearly every major car manufacturer has at least one green vehicle in their inventory. We're relatively sure that as alternative fuels become more and more popular because of the cost and the positive effects on our environment, the number of green vehicles will dramatically increase in the next few years.

As of 2006, here is a list of some of the green vehicles manufactured by some of the major car companies:

- Honda Insight
- Honda Accord Hybrid
- Dodge Ram Pickup 1500 Series
- Dodge Stratus Sedan
- Dodge Durango SUV
- Dodge Caravan Minivan
- Ford Taurus
- Ford F-150 Pickup
- Ford Escape SUV
- GM Impala
- Chevrolet Silverado 4 x 2
- Chevrolet Tahoe SUV
- Chevy Yukon SUV
- Nissan Titan Pickup
- Toyota Highlander SUV
- Toyota Prius

Energy Conservation And Alternative Fuel

Many of the vehicles listed above are hybrid vehicles which mean that they can run on both conventional gasoline as well as alternative fuels. As we said, the above list is for 2006 vehicles. The list for 2007 is much larger.

There are also two other types of AFVs that are becoming more and more popular. First, there is the electric vehicle. This car is exactly what it says it is. You plug it into an electrical outlet to charge the battery and then drive without using any fuel at all. However, these vehicles are generally not meant to travel at high speeds.

A second type of AFV is the fuel cell vehicle. These cars get electrical energy from a fuel cell instead of from a battery. There are different kinds of fuel cell vehicles, but most manufacturers prefer cells that use a proton exchange membrane that uses hydrogen to produce an electrical current to run the motor. The only type of exhaust with this type of vehicle is water – believe it or not!

Besides the obvious advantages to owning an AFV, the government is also stepping in to make it even more advantageous. People who buy these types of vehicles are given tax breaks on their income taxes. Additionally, many states also offer incentives and car manufacturers even offer rebates or discounts.

Gasoline And Oil

In the United States and the rest of the industrialized world, gasoline is definitely a vital fluid. It is as vital to the economy as blood is to a person. Without gasoline and diesel fuel, the world as we know it would grind to a halt. The U.S. alone consumes about 130 billion gallons of gasoline per year!

This could get a little technical here, but we think it's important. Gasoline is known as an aliphatic hydrocarbon. In other words, gasoline is made up of molecules composed of nothing but hydrogen and carbon arranged in chains. Gasoline molecules have from seven to 11 carbons in each chain.

When you burn gasoline under ideal conditions – meaning with plenty of oxygen - you get carbon dioxide from the carbon atoms in gasoline, water from the hydrogen atoms, and lots of heat. A gallon of gasoline contains about 132×10^6 joules of energy, which is equivalent to 125,000 BTU or 36,650 watt-hours.

To illustrate this concept, consider the following:

- If you took a 1,500-watt space heater and left it on full blast for a full 24-hour day, that's about how much heat is in a gallon of gas.

- If it were possible for human beings to digest gasoline, a gallon would contain about 31,000 food calories -- the energy in a gallon of gasoline is equivalent to the energy in about 110 McDonald's hamburgers!

Now, stick with us through this next part! It can get a little confusing!

Gasoline is made from crude oil. The crude oil pumped out of the ground is black liquid called petroleum. This liquid contains hydrocarbons, and the carbon atoms in crude oil link together in chains of different lengths.

It turns out that hydrocarbon molecules of different lengths have different properties and behaviors. For example, a chain with just one carbon atom in it (CH_4) is the lightest chain, known as methane. Methane is a gas so light that it floats like helium. As the chains get longer, they get heavier.

The first four chains -- CH_4 (methane), C_2H_6 (ethane), C_3H_8 (propane) and C_4H_{10} (butane) -- are all gases, and they boil at -161, -88, -46 and -1 degrees F, respectively, The chains up through $C_{18}H_{32}$ or so are all liquids at room temperature, and the chains above C_{19} are all solids – such as fats - at room temperature.

The different chain lengths have progressively higher boiling points, so they can be separated out by distillation. This is what happens in an oil refinery -- crude oil is heated and the different chains are pulled out by their vaporization temperatures.

The chains in the C5, C6 and C7 range are all very light, easily vaporized, clear liquids called naphthas. They are used as solvents. Cleaning products can be made from these liquids, as well as paint solvents and other quick-drying products.

Environmental Damage

It took over 200 million years for the oil beneath the earth's surface to form. In the past 200 years, we have already used half of that reserve. If current rates of consumption continue, the world's remaining oil would be used up in 40 years.

Right now, two-thirds of the oil used around the world powers transportation vehicles, and half goes to passenger cars and light trucks. Being conscious of our fuel use will help to conserve resources for future generations.

Transportation involves the combustion of fossil fuels to produce energy translated into motion. Pollution is created from incomplete carbon reactions, unburned hydrocarbons or other elements present in the fuel or air during combustion.

These processes produce pollutants of various species, including carbon monoxide, soot, various gaseous and liquid vapor hydrocarbons, oxides of sulphur and nitrogen, sulphate and nitrate particulates, ash and lead. These primary pollutants can, in turn, react in the atmosphere to form ozone, secondary particulates, and other damaging secondary pollutants. Combustion also produces carbon dioxide, the primary greenhouse gas.

These environmental concerns about the country's transportation habits have been studied extensively. The tailpipe emissions from cars and trucks account for almost a third of the air pollution in the United States.

Although smog is produced by many factors, including sunlight, temperatures, winds and "basin" effects the air pollution caused by transportation is a major contributor. In their Sprawl Report 2001, the Sierra Club graded the car and truck smog in America's 50 largest cities using data from the EPA.

The area containing New York City scored best, believe it or not, with a grade of C+, creating 54 pounds of smog from cars and trucks per person per year. Twelve of the top 50 cities earned a grade of F, including, surprisingly, Louisville, Kentucky, which has 137 pounds of smog from cars and trucks per person per year.

The Clean Air Act of 1970 gave the U.S. Environmental Protection Agency broad authority to regulate motor vehicle pollution, and since then, emission control policies have become progressively more stringent. In addition, the EPA has published various fact sheets, such as "Your Car and Clean Air: What YOU Can Do to Reduce Pollution."

Global Warming

Former Vice President of the United States, Al Gore, has brought the issue of global warming to the forefront of people's minds with his Oscar winning documentary, "An Inconvenient Truth." While there are some people who have been concerned about global warming for years, but this movie helped make the phenomenon more "famous" if you will.

If you've never thought about global warming, consider the following facts:

·Since the 1970's, there has been a 100 percent increase in the intensity and duration of hurricanes and tropical storms.

·According to the U.S. Geological Survey predictions, by the year 2030, Glacier National Park will have no glaciers left at all.

·400,000 square miles of the Arctic Sea have melted in the last thirty years. That is roughly the size of Texas and is threatening polar bear habitats.

·By the year 2050, 15 to 17 percent of animal and plant species will be wiped out by global warming

·The United States is the number one global warming polluter in the world.

·Six former United States Environmental Protection Agency leaders say that the U.S. isn't doing enough to reduce pollution that contributes to global warming. This is supported by the fact that the United States Congress has not passed one piece of legislation related to the reduction of global warming.

Basically, global warming is an observable progressive warming of the average temperature of the Earth over a period of time. While some people might think is a great thing envisioning mild winters, but the truth is that global warming is a disturbing phenomenon.

The rising temperatures can cause changes like rising sea levels, an increase in the frequency and intensity of severe weather, decreased agricultural yields, and glacial retreats and/or disappearances. Global warming is also projected to cause the eventual extinction of many plant and animal species as they struggle to survive in warmer climates that they aren't used to.

Global warming is caused mostly by the release of methane gas into the environment. Methane is a greenhouse gas that traps heat in the Earth's atmosphere. Methane gas is naturally released from arctic tundra and wetlands.

However, the biggest contributing factors toward global warming are man-made. Man-made causes bring about the most damage when considering the global warming trend.

Pollution is one of the biggest man-made problems. Pollution comes in many shapes and sizes. Burning fossil fuels is one thing that causes pollution. Fossil fuels are fuels made of organic matter such as coal, or oil. When fossil fuels are burned they give off a green house gas called carbon dioxide (CO_2).

Alternative Fuel According To The Numbers

Is it any cheaper to produce alternative fuels? The answer is simply - sometimes.

Ethanol

Ethanol, as we've already addressed is basically 85 percent grain alcohol and 15 percent gasoline. It is a cleaner burning fuel and provides more horsepower than gasoline alone. While ethanol burns cooler than gasoline, it doesn't provide enough power to get an engine started on cold days which is why gasoline is added to the mixture.

With the rising popularity of E85 gasoline, more vehicles are being produced that can accommodate this new fuel. E85 fueling stations are currently available in 36 states (as of 2006), and over 6 million vehicles that can use E85 have been sold.

The performance of E85 vehicles is potentially higher than that of gasoline vehicles because E85's high octane rating allows a much higher compression ratio, which translates into higher thermodynamic efficiency. However, the flex-fuel vehicles (FFVs) that retain the capacity to run on gasoline alone can't really take advantage of this octane boost since they also need to be able to run on pump-grade gasoline.

Methanol

Methanol is wood alcohol and, like ethanol, is blended in an 85/15 blend with gasoline. Methanol is produced through a steam and catalyst process that reconstitutes methane gas as methanol.

We know that methane gas is one of the primary causes of global warming and environmental degradation, but the way methane is processed into methanol safely turns it into safer methane. That safer methane can power vehicles with considerably less damage to the environment than methane by itself.

Currently, virtually all methanol produced in the United States uses methane derived from natural gas. However, methane also can be obtained from coal and from biogas, which is generated by fermenting organic matter--including byproducts of sewage and manure.

On a positive note, methanol is a potent fuel with an octane rating of 100 that allows for higher compression and greater efficiency than gasoline. Pure methanol isn't volatile enough to start a cold engine easily and when it does burn, it does so with a dangerously invisible flame. Blending gasoline with methanol to create M85 solves both problems.

Compressed Natural Gas

Natural gas can be used to fuel internal-combustion engines. The most practical strategy is to handle it as compressed natural gas (CNG).

Natural gas is typically found in underground deposits, often with petroleum, and is obtained by drilling. To use natural gas, the methane component--which makes up 50 to 100 percent of natural gas--must be processed to remove contaminants as well as other useful fuels such as butane and propane.

With an octane rating of up to 130, CNG has the potential to optimize an engine's thermodynamic efficiency through a high compression ratio. However, many CNG vehicles are able to run on either CNG or gasoline, which makes the octane advantage obvious.

According to the DOE, a CNG-fueled Honda Civic GX--the sole widely available CNG-only vehicle in the United States--produces 90 percent less CO and 60 percent less nitrogen oxides (NOx) than its gas-powered counterpart. And, CO_2 is reduced by 30 to 40 percent. According to the company, the car's exhaust is cleaner than the air in some high-pollution areas.

For a vehicle to carry enough CNG to travel a reasonable distance, the gas has to be compressed to 3000 to 3600 psi (pounds per inch). At 3600 psi, CNG has about one-third as much energy as gasoline--about 44,000 BTU per unit volume--and the tank must be far larger, heavier and more expensive than a conventional one.

Energy Conservation Throughout the Home

In each area of your home you can conserve energy. If you are looking for a few extra dollars to fall off of your home energy bill this month, consider the tips that you find here. To get started, consider your water heater. The water heater is a key element within a home. It is also one of the many elements that are often overlooked when it comes to energy conservation. If you want to actually make some money on its usage, consider adjusting how you use it.

The first thing that you should do is adjust the heater dial. You should keep the thermostat set absolutely no lower than 120 degrees F. If you go lower than this, you run the risk of sanitation issues. Of course, if you prefer the water to be hotter, then increase it. But, consider this. If you do not take a shower on full blast hot water, you are using cold water to cool down the hot water that you just paid a considerable amount of money to heat up. Lowering the dial will help to keep the amount that you need to heat it up down.

In addition to that, you can save a great deal of money keeping the water in the hot water heater hot. To do this, insulate your water tank. Most of the modern hot water tanks offer some insulation inside of them. But, adding a protective layer of insulation outside of them will also make them beneficial to your energy needs. You can purchase water heater insulation covers that will easily fit right over them to lock in the heat. Take care to put these on correctly.

Saving money on the amount of hot water that you use is vitally important for energy conservation. Take a few minutes now to find out what your water heater is set at. Determine if you have the potential for saving money here.

Energy Conservation Through Your Piping

Energy conservation is something that must be done throughout the home. One additional consideration that you should look into is your piping. The home has a huge piping network in it that allows water to be pumped throughout the home. If your hot water heater is located on one side of the home and the bathroom is located on the other, then there is the potential for a good amount of water to be lost in this movement. Yet, this does not have to be so. If you can save some energy here it is through protecting the piping.

Find out how to access the piping that runs from your hot water heater. After you have insulated the hot water heater itself, you can then move on to insulating the piping that runs throughout your home. Do not worry, though, this is not as large of a task as you may have thought. A trip to the local hardware store will result in piping insulation. This insulation is cut to fit snuggling around the piping. All you need to do is to snap it around the piping neatly. Be careful at the edges not to make any tears. Once in place, use duct tape to seal off any edges surrounding the insulation.

Once you have the piping within your home insulated, you can begin to see some energy conservation. Now, as the hot water moves from the actual hot water tank to the faucet in your bathroom, it moves without losing as much heat. In the process, when the water finally gets to you, it is hot as it comes out. You do not need to pump up the faucet higher to get hotter water because it is still as hot as I was when it left the tank. The end result is energy conservation.

Energy Conservation With Your Furnace

The furnace is a major player in the home. If you are one that enjoys the heat in the winter (as if we didn't!) you need to have a furnace that is properly working. Yet, there is much more to it than that. Just because your furnace turns on this winter does not mean that it is running at the highest level that it could. If you do not have someone come out to check your furnace each year before it becomes cold outdoors, do so. It is an investment you will not soon forget. But, what can you do to conserve energy from this point? There are actually several things to consider.

First of all, taking proper care of your furnace will work wonders on the quality of heat that you get. If your thermostat is calling for heat and the furnace is trying to push the heat out into the home but it cannot get there because the air ducts or the furnace filter is dirty and dusty, then it must keep calling for heat which will not only cost you a considerable amount of money but it will also lead to a very unhealthy furnace and one that will not last as long.

Besides keeping your furnace clean and working well, the next thing for you to do is to use a programmable thermostat. This can control the amount of heat that comes into the home when you need it. There is no sense in heating a home that is always empty from nine to five everyday. Have the furnace kick on a few hours before you get home. A key here is to have the thermostat set at different settings for the day and night too. By doing these things they will help make sure that energy conservation is what your furnace is capable of.

Energy Conservation Outdoors

Outside the home, there are some things that you can do to find benefits on your energy bill. Although most think about only the ways to save money inside the home, outdoors there are many things that can be done to benefit your overall energy usage. It only takes a few minutes to consider these tips. While these tips for outdoor energy conservation are likely to cost more to install and maintain then indoors, they can offer quite a bit of benefit nevertheless and therefore should be considered. To get started, think about this.

- **Trees:** Trees provide a great deal of shade for your home. They can lower the temperature of your home by up to three percent if they are placed correctly around the home. Shading three to four sides of the home drops your air conditioning's workload, saving you a good amount of money in the process.
- **Wind breakers.** Consider installing fencing or even just shrubs around the home. When you do this, the wind does not slam into the home. The benefit here is that you do not have cold air dropping the temperature of your home as quickly. It can help to lower the heating needs that you have a good deal especially in very windy locations.
- **Water Drainage.** While you want water to always drain away from your home, you can have well designed landscaping that will keep water draining into the soil for the plants and grass to use. You do not want the water to just go into the drain.
- **Consider solar powered lighting outdoors as well.** Here, the lighting stores the energy during the day and then will power lights at night long after the sun has gone down. This is free energy, after all.

Outdoors, you can save money with energy conservation. You just need to know how to do it.

Energy Conservation Tips To Get Started

Energy conservation is something you just have to invest in. If you do not do so, you are harming the environment and you are keeping the cost of fuel very high. Any of us can benefit by using a few of these tips to help us to shave the costs of energy within our homes and even in the business. Which will you do first?

1. **Check windows and repair as needed.** As one of the largest energy losses, it is necessary to consider this need as one the first priorities on your list.
2. **Check your water heater.** Is it set at the lowest possible comfortable and sanitary setting? It is insulated for optimum benefit? Doing these things will insure that your water heater is working at its best for energy savings.
3. **As your light bulbs burn out, switch to florescent Energy Star light bulbs.** These will last you quite a long while. They will also use less than half of the amount of energy to light your room. Don't do this all at once, but slowly as needed.
4. **Turn off anything that you can.** Lower the settings on ceiling fans. Keep the lights off and the LED lights throughout your home off as well. These things may seem little but they do add up quickly.
5. **Plant a few trees and shrubs outdoors to help break the wind and keep your home cool during the summer.** During the winter, shrubs help to insulate your home by keeping the cold air out.

These are just a few of the things that you can use to conserve energy. The best thing to do to make this happen is to involve your whole family. Once habits are learned about these things, you all can save a good deal of money on energy. The end result is that you get more money in your pocket and the Earth stays a bit healthier as a result of energy conservation.

Electric Car Conversions

Odds are, you probably own a gasoline or diesel powered vehicle. If you are considering making the switch to an electric car, there are some things you should consider before getting started.

Should I Buy a New Vehicle?

If you are in the market for an electric car, the easiest option is to simply go new car shopping. There are a few production electric cars out there right now. Be aware that while an electric car is more expensive up front, if it suits your commuting needs you can save a lot of money in the long run on fuel costs. Most production electric cars have more limited range than a gasoline vehicle, but as long as you don't drive more than 50 miles on a daily basis, they will be just fine. Along with the electric car, you will usually receive a power station for your home, where you plug your car in to recharge overnight. Remember, power isn't free, and has to come from somewhere. You can expect a rise in your electricity bill, but usually you are still saving money over a gasoline vehicle. And check the laws in the state you live in! California, for instance, offers some very nice incentives to owners of green alternative fuel vehicles. This includes electrically powered vehicles.

Converting Your Existing Vehicle

If you just don't want to give up your gas guzzlers style or storage capacity, it is possible to convert your vehicle to run on electricity. Just be aware from the get go that this is an expensive project that is definitely not a do-it-yourself deal. Pretty much every active component of your vehicle will have to be replaced with versions designed for electric vehicles. But the costs will probably not be much more than purchasing an electric vehicle, and you may like the results much better.

Get in touch with some companies that specialize in alternative energy sources, such as solar power or fuel cells. Even if they can't help you with your specific project, they can probably point you towards someone that can. The company that you finally settle on will have quite a few issues to discuss with you, such as the battery types, or whether to go pure electric, or hybrid. Electricity-generating fuel cells are another option, but can be expensive to maintain. There are many different ways to go when talking electric car conversions, and many need to be worked out with someone who knows what is what.

It's All Worth It

But once you actually perform the conversion, you will be amazed at the difference. Electric vehicles are nearly silent, and you'll never have to pump gas again. They have a very futuristic feel about them, with computerized systems and displays as finishing touches. And they produce no emissions whatsoever, so you are doing a major favor to the environment. Imagine how much less smog there would be in your city if everyone drove zero emission electric cars.

Direct Methanol Fuel Cell

The Direct Methanol Fuel Cell is, at its core, just a fuel cell. It converts fuel into electricity without producing all the harmful byproducts of combustion. How is it different than any other fuel cell? Let's take a quick look at how other fuel cells operate.

Gasoline Fuel Cells

Most petrochemical fuel cells require the fuel to go through a complicated (and expensive) catalyzation processes before finally being fed into the fuel cell final chamber for conversion to electricity. This raises the costs mainly due to the expensive materials needed as catalysts in the fuel cell. And the catalytic elements require routine maintenance to continue operating at good efficiency.

Hydrogen Fuel Cells

Hydrogen fuel cells, on the other hand, don't require this expensive catalyzing process. The hydrogen can be fed directly into the core, just as it is with direct methanol fuel cells. But the basic problem with a hydrogen fuel cell is the same as with any other hydrogen-based energy generation: hydrogen is dangerous and difficult to store, requiring high pressures and low temperatures to remain in liquid form; the gaseous form has too low an energy density (defined as potential energy per unit of volume) to be practical.

The Direct Methanol Fuel Cell

The direct methanol fuel cell takes the low costs, direct-injection advantages of the hydrogen fuel cell, and couples it with the high energy density and high liquification temperature of petrochemicals. Because of this, methanol is an excellent alternative to both hydrogen and gasoline fuel cells. At least, it could be.

Limitations of the Direct Methanol Fuel Cell

The biggest problem with direct methanol fuel cells is their relatively low efficiency due to membrane permeation by the methanol, This phenomenon is called methanol crossover, and leads to sluggish responses to dynamic power requirement changes. In other words, if you stomp the accelerator, your car would be sluggish to respond due to the cell taking time to "ramp up" to the new required levels. There are also problems with managing the carbon dioxide produced as waste gas.

These problems make the methanol fuel cell a better choice for low power, long duration applications, such as personal electronics, cell phones, laptops, and the like. But with more time and research, direct methanol fuel cells could be a good solution to our current alternative fuel crisis. Cheaper to produce than gasoline fuel cells, much safer than hydrogen, and currently available for purchase, these direct methanol fuel cells may just be the wave of the future.

Fuel Cells For Small Household Appliances

Fuel cell technology and research has come a long way since the early days. Fuel cells used to be large, bulky, and expensive to build and maintain. But this new generation is any but big and bulky. In fact, it is now possible to build fuel cells small enough to power nearly any small household appliance.

Fuel Cells for Everyday Use

With the development of these new small fuel cells could come a major evolution in portable power sources for small household appliances. Because fuel cells can now be made that are small and lightweight, they can make nearly any small appliance in your house cordless. I'm sure you can easily see the advantages of that!

Developing the Small Fuel Cell

While these types of applications were not exactly what the pioneers of fuel cell research had in mind, they are a natural offspring of the desire to make smaller, lighter, and more efficient fuel cell designs. First targeted towards green vehicles, researchers quickly realized that fuel cells could provide more power for a longer period of time than any battery technology currently available. This led to research towards putting fuel cells into cell phones and laptops - both products that use relatively large amounts of power and require a power source that is both small and light, and provides plenty of reserve electricity. A miniature fuel cell fits these requirements perfectly. The energy density obtainable using a liquid fuel source far exceeds even the best batteries in the same amount of space.

Marketing to the Consumer

While initially seen as a niche application by most of the small household appliance industry, the growing trend towards cordless technologies in all sorts of applications has led to research into fuel cells aimed at devices larger than portable electronics, but smaller than the cells a vehicle requires. The vacuum cleaner, for example, is a prime candidate for small house appliance fuel cell technology. The benefits of a cordless vacuum cleaner are obvious, but until now, cordless models have had to have much smaller motors than their corded brethren. That 12 amp motor in your corded vacuum would drain current battery technologies dry in short order. But fuel cells, with their much higher energy density, allow for full sized cordless vacuums to be built.

Just Around the Corner

With such obvious applications and ever-decreasing costs to manufacture fuel cells, expect to see fuel cell powered versions of many small household appliances in the near future. If the success of the laptop fuel cell is any indication, fuel cells could very well be the next big thing.

Alternative Fuel Vehicles

Green Vehicles - Pushing Alternative Fuel Vehicles

In the last couple of years, there has been growing pressure both from the general public and from government agencies pushing for more use of alternative fuels for your daily commute. The reasoning behind this is easy to understand: amidst dwindling oil supplies, increasing numbers of vehicles on the roads, and a more environmentally aware population, alternative fuel vehicles offer an alternative to increasingly expensive and polluting gasoline or diesel. But any vehicle can't just pull into the hydrogen or ethanol station and immediately run on that fuel. Engines and the systems that control them must be redesigned to use alternative fuels.

So Where Can I Get One?

Nowadays, most manufacturers are building at least a couple alternative fuel vehicles. No manufacturer wants to be the dinosaur that didn't adapt, and even if the fuels are not yet widely available for some types of alternative fuel vehicles, the vehicles themselves are available now. Some alternative fuel vehicles are designed to run on pure alternatives to gasoline, others take a "hybrid" approach and use gasoline either in new and cleaner ways (such as fuel cells) or use a mix of gasoline and other alternative fuels (gasohol, for example).

As of the year 2006, these are some alternative fuel vehicles produced by major car manufacturers:

Chevrolet Silverado 4x2
Chevrolet Tahoe SUV
Chevrolet Yukon SUV
Dodge Caravan Minivan
Dodge Durango SUV
Dodge Ram Pickup 1500 Series
Dodge Stratus Sedan
Ford Escape SUV
Ford F-150 Pickup

Energy Conservation And Alternative Fuel

Ford Taurus
GM Impala
Honda Accord Hybrid
Honda Insight
Nissan Titan Pickup
Toyota Highlander SUV
Toyota Prius

These are just a sampling of the various alternative fuel vehicles available on the market now. More and more alternative fuel vehicles are being designed and produced every year. Environmentally friendly is the only way to go in today's climate of environmental awareness. Entire alternative fuel infrastructures are being designed (and implemented, as in Honda's rollout of hydrogen refueling stations in California this year).

Cost of Owning Your Alternative Fuel Vehicle

As of right now, alternative fuel vehicles generally have a higher sticker price than a similar gasoline powered vehicle. As an environmentally-conscious consumer, you can expect to pay anywhere from $3000-$10,000 more for your alternative fuel vehicle. But don't despair, this is exactly why some states are offering tax breaks, reimbursements, and other incentives to consumers and businesses that purchase and use alternative fuel vehicles. California, Texas, and Florida, for instance, have an exemption for alternative fuel vehicles. Many of you are familiar with the "Carpool", "High-Occupancy", and similar lanes on your cities bypasses. These are usually reserved for cars that are carrying more than 1 or 2 people to work. Well, if you are driving your alternative fuel vehicle, you can use these lanes even when you are all by yourself! The US Federal government is offering tax breaks to people who purchased and alternative fuel vehicle this year. For some people, especially business owners and the self-employed, these vehicles can offer a sizable tax reduction that is well worth the initial investment in your alternative fuel vehicle.

Alternative Fuel History

Alternative fuels, or at least the concept of them, have been around since the early days of the automobile. The gasoline internal combustion engine changed the face of the planet, but since day 1 people have looked for other fuels to power this engine with.

It wasn't until the American gas shortages of the 1970's that research into alternative fuels really began in earnest. Faced with shortages of gasoline, there was no choice but to develop some alternatives to the standard gasoline engine. What they discovered was ethanol.

Ethanol

Alcohol made from corn has been around since mankind first learned to cultivate it, but it wasn't until the 70's that scientists realized it could be used in gasoline powered vehicles. Ethanol (denatured with enough methanol that people couldn't drink it) could power an internal combustion engine as effectively as petrochemicals, but without a lot of the harmful byproducts of petrochemical combustion. It was cheaper to make than gasoline, and would require large amounts of corn, which was good for the farmers at the time.

There were other fuels that were discovered to work as well, with modifications to the engine to accommodate the new fuels. Natural gas, propane, and hydrogen will all power an internal combustion engine just as well as gasoline or ethanol. But there were (and still are) problems with fuel storage and delivery, and the engine must be modified to use these fuels - they won't work in a standard gasoline engine design.

Why Aren't We Using Alternative Fuels Then?

There is probably no simple answer as to why we aren't already using these alternative fuels now - 30 years after research first began. Some cite the political clout of the big oil companies, others cite the expense of changing the infrastructure to a new fuel type (which is made all the more difficult by the millions of gasoline vehicles already on the roads), still others say that the technologies simply are not ready yet. The true answer probably lies with a blending of all these reasons and many more - societal inertia comes to mind. People are simply comfortable with there gas guzzlers, and until a good portion of the population wants this change, it won't happen. But fortunately, this is occurring today. With gas prices spiraling up out of control at the pump, more and more cities cloaked in a thickening layer of smog, and global environmental awareness hitting its peak, popular demand for alternative fuels that are cheaper and greener is at an all-time high.

Alternative Fuel Hummer

Ever since the military released the Humvee design to the open market, it has been a favorite vehicle for many people. General Motors produces this amored truck turned luxury vehicle, and have recently announce a version made to run on biodiesel.

Gas-Guzzling Vehicles

The Hummer has long been a favorite target of environmentalists and conservationists worldwide because of its famously atrocious gas mileage. The Hummer uses more fuel than 5 economy vehicles, and that means 5 times as much smog and carbon dioxide, a greenhouse gas. It only makes sense to try and minimize the amount of harmful byproducts this monster vehicle produces, and biodiesel may be a big step towards a solution.

Biodiesel and Pollution

Biodiesel is a natural alternative to petroleum-based diesel and can be used in most diesel engines without any modifications needed. It is completely biodegradable and is non-toxic. However, some engines do require optimization to be able to run on 100% biodiesel. Most unmodified diesel engines will run on a mixture of petroleum and biodiesel with no problems. Bio diesel, when used alone, produces 65% less smog-causing emissions than regular diesel, and around 60% less carbon dioxide emissions. All this while maintaining the same fuel efficiency as petroleum-based diesel.

Pioneering the Alternative-Fuel Hummer

The man who made it happen is Tom Holm and the non-profit Eco-Trek Foundation. While most environmental groups bemoan the Hummer, this group decided to do something about it. Tim's alternative fuel Hummer runs on B100 (that's 100 percent biodiesel) and gets 23 miles per gallon. That means that this Hummer produces less carbon dioxide and smog than any petroleum economy vehicle, while promoting the use of the environmentally friendly alternative fuels.

Biodiesel Isn't The Only Game In Town

But there is another alternative to even a biodiesel alternative fuel Hummer: one that runs on the environmentalist's favorite fuel: hydrogen. Arnold Schwarzenegger owns this Hummer, which is not widely available yet. Hydrogen produces absolutely no emissions other than water vapor, making it by far the cleanest alternative fuel hummer available. But the availability of hydrogen is still quite limited, and for the moment it is far more expensive than biodiesel. It requires a complete engine reworking to run on pure hydrogen, and special fuel storage considerations. Biodiesel, on the other hand, is easily distributed by the same channels as petroleum products, and does not require very much, if any, engine reworking.

Environmentally Friendly and Renewable

No matter what car you drive, you should look into a biodiesel or other alternative fuel replacement. Biodiesel is a renewable resource (unlike petroleum), and is far cleaner and less hazardous than any petroleum product. These vehicles may be more expensive now, but someday you will be chuckling as you pay half what the pure petroleum users are paying. As petroleum prices rise, pressure to make the switch to alternative, cheaper fuel is as well. It is only a matter of time before alternative fuel vehicles become the norm, rather than the exception.

Alternative Hydrogen Fuel Made On Site

Probably the single most promising alternative fuel we have to date is also one of the most abundant elements on the planet: plain old hydrogen. Hydrogen can be made cheaply and easily on site anywhere there is a ready source of water and electricity. That means no more American dependence on foreign oil for our energy needs, and lower fuel costs while cleaning up smog and other pollution.

How a Hydrogen Plant Works

Hydrogen is not found in any significant quantity as a free gas on Earth. As the lightest of all the elements, what free hydrogen there once was has long since boiled away into space. All that remain now are minute quantities of free hydrogen in the upper atmosphere. Most of Earths hydrogen is locked away in the form of water.

A hydrogen plant, therefore, makes hydrogen on site by a simple process known as electrolysis. What this boils down to is simply this: when you pass an electric current through water, it breaks apart into hydrogen and oxygen gases. The gases are collected, separated, and compressed into liquid form. And that's all there is to it!

Hydrogen Storage and Transport

The single biggest problem is that hydrogen is dangerous to store and transport. Since it liquefies at extremely low temperatures and high pressures, the safety concerns are considerable. For this reason alone, we will probably never see liquid hydrogen powering our personal vehicles. Rather, hydrogen can be used to generate electricity at central power stations which is then used to charge an electric vehicle. But it cannot be said with any certainty that this is the only way it will work. There are some promising developments in cell storage, where the liquid hydrogen is stored in an aero gel foam that is immune to catastrophic failure due to heating or ruptures. The hydrogen gas is allowed to bubble up out of the foam for the fuel cell or hydrogen combustion engine.

The Benefits of Hydrogen

Hydrogen as a fuel, whether used in fuel cells or simply burned in a combustion engine, is manifold. There are absolutely no emissions other than water vapor, which returns to the ground as rain, ready to be reformed into hydrogen gas for burning again. Contrast this to the limited petroleum resources we have available, in non-renewable deposits, and all the harmful byproducts of petrochemical combustion. It certainly seems that hydrogen will someday be powering our cities, vehicles, and maybe even our electronics with miniaturized fuel cells producing electricity. A greener world is not as far off as you may think!

Types Of Alternative Fuels

With pollution an increasingly important concern as worldwide energy consumption continues to rise, research into alternative fuel is at an all time high. Here are some of the currently available alternative fuels, and what's still to come.

Alcohol Fuels

Probably the most widespread alternative fuel is ethanol. Ethanol is just plain old grain alcohol, made from corn or soybeans. There aren't very many vehicles at the moment that can run on pure ethanol. Most of the time, what is available are ethanol blends, which is just ethanol blended with varying percentages of gasoline. At this time, the highest percentage available is 85 percent ethanol, 15 percent gasoline.

Methanol is also used, but is not as common as ethanol. Methanol is also called wood alcohol, and can be produced from wood fermentation or from coal, but is usually made more cheaply from natural gas.

Natural Gas Fuels

Another alternative fuel is natural gas. This petroleum-based gas burns more cleanly than gasoline, but still suffers from the renewability problems of all petroleum products. It is also an actual gas, unlike liquid propane, and thus suffers from storage issues. Propane is the alternative, and is a liquid when stored, but still suffers from renewability problems.

Electricity

Electricity is the focus of much research, because it is not tied (from the consumers' point of view) to any particular fuel source and produces zero emissions at the vehicle. This shifts the burden of utilizing cleaner, often harder-to-handle fuels, away from the average end user and into the hands of organizations with the resources to safely handle the alternative fuels. The main problem with using electricity is, again, storage. Current batteries often require large banks to provide enough power for reasonable speeds and distances. For this reason, electricity is still more often found in "hybrid" vehicles that use petroleum products to generate extra electricity when needed.

Hydrogen - The Holy Grail of Alternative Fuels

Hydrogen is the most promising alternative fuel source currently under development. It is extremely clean, producing only water vapor as an emission, and is one of the most abundant elements on the planet in the form of water. All that is needed to produce hydrogen is a source of electricity to separate water into hydrogen and oxygen. The biggest drawback is that hydrogen is only liquid at extremely low temperatures, and extremely explosive when mixed with air in gaseous form. These characteristics make hydrogen hard to safely store and transport, especially in an end-user safe fashion.

These are only a sampling of the various types of alternative fuels available or under development. With petroleum prices skyrocketing, pressure to develop an alternative fuel fit for mass consumption is at an all-time high. Many other possible alternative fuels are being developed and studied every day. In the end, the mass use of these fuels will result in an overall better quality of life on this planet.

Alternative Energy For The Home

There is a growing trend in today's world towards using cleaner, greener, and most importantly, renewable resources. It is no longer a question of if we run out of oil, only when. And people are already feeling the pinch every time they gas up at the pump or get the latest gas bill.

The result of this trend has been more and more home owners looking into alternative energy sources to run their household on. This is both a necessary step in our evolution as a society and a sound economic choice for home owners today. What are some of the methods that can be used to power a home today? Let's take a look at a few of the more common choices.

Solar Power

Everything on the planet runs on the energy provided by our sun. The oil your car runs on is nothing more than stored solar energy, when you get right down to it. So the move to solar power just makes sense. Solar power can be used in a few different ways. It is possible to run a home directly off of your solar panels, and rely on the power company to provide electricity when the sun is down or on cloudy days. When your solar panels are operating, you feed any energy you are not using at the moment back through your meter into the power grid. This has the effect of actually making your meter run backwards during the day. Hopefully, either you will produce more during the day than you use at night, or at least break even. The second and most common method of using solar power is to simply have your solar panels charge a large bank of batteries that your house then draws power from. Again, any excess energy produced can be fed back and sold to the power company, with electricity from the grid making up any shortfalls. The third way of utilizing solar power is somewhat more complex, and is probably not currently applicable to the average home owner. Using solar power to break down water into hydrogen and oxygen, you can store solar energy in much the same way as oil does, and release it later by combustion or fuel cells. This is really only feasible right for the power companies, but has the advantage of storing up excess solar energy in a form that can be used on cloudy days, ensuring an uninterrupted flow of power.

Wind Power

This alternative energy source is best used in conjunction with the solar power methods described above. In stormy weather, for instance, the sun may be hidden, but the wind may be blowing hard, and vice-versa for sunny days. This can help smooth out the available alternative energy levels available, and lead to more power being sold to the power company.

Hydroelectric Power

Most people would probably not think of hydroelectric power as a viable source of alternative energy for their home, but if you have access to a source of running water like a creek, you can generate a surprisingly large amount of power with only a small dam. When used either in conjunction with solar and wind, or on its own, hydroelectric power can easily completely replace the power company as the source of power in a home.

Heating Water Using Solar Power

Whether you are converting your whole home to run on solar power, or simply looking to save some money and help the environment at the same time, you should seriously consider using solar power to heat your water. These system can either completely replace or supplement you existing hot water system.

There are a few of different ways you can use solar power to heat your water. Let's take a look at some of the more common ways of heating water using solar power.

The first involves using your existing electric hot water heater, and powering it via your household solar power system. This can work, but hot water heaters draw large amounts of electricity, can leave the rest of your house starving for energy, and can put a strain on your batteries. Most solar power system in most places in the US will have a hard time keeping up with the demands of an electric hot water heater doing all the work on its own.

The second method involves piping your water through coils in solar collectors (basically reflective boxes that focus the sun's heat energy onto the water pipes). This method has the advantage of using no electricity on its own, but can take up roof space that could be used to generate more electricity. But the total energy saved is most often worth the slight drop in electrical power generation.

Perhaps the most efficient method involves using a somewhat hybrid approach, in which water is heated by passing through the solar collectors, and is piped down and stored in an electric water heater that is run either off of solar power or the existing electrical grid. It takes much less energy to maintain hot water in an insulated container via electricity than it does to heat it entirely with the same electricity.

In all cases, there will be special installations required. Controls for the solar collectors to keep the water from getting too hot, extra water storage tanks for water that is being heated on the roof, and the solar panels and associated electrical systems if also converting to solar electrical power. But with a little time and research invested, you can do most of the installation yourself. An electrician will always be required to do the final connections to the power grid, however.

There are several safety devices that must be in place to protect people working on the power lines, and most power companies require certification before they will allow a consumer to hook a solar power system into the grid.

While these system can be expensive to set up, they will quickly pay for themselves in saved energy bills. Some states also offer generous tax or cash incentives for home owners willing to go green. Some states will even help pay for the system initially! With all the concern over renewable non-polluting energy sources, there has never been a better time to go solar.

Electric Car Facts

When it comes to one of the newest developments in the vehicle industry – electric cars – the facts about them are plentiful and easy to come by. This new alternative to regular gasoline powered cars has many people very excited about being able to have reliable transportation without damaging the environment. So what are the facts about electric cars?

First, there are many types of electric cars you can choose from, but all of them use an electric motor that runs on batteries that you recharge. The more batteries you have, the longer you can drive your car. Electric cars come in all different sizes and performances. They are aerodynamically more efficient than gasoline powered cars because electricity stored chemically is lighter than electricity stored electrically.

Another very advantageous fact about electric cars is that they emit virtually no greenhouse gases into the air and thus run much, much cleaner than many other vehicles. Greenhouse gases contribute to the depletion of the ozone layer that has led to global warming. Electric cars that run on batteries alone produce no pollution at all and thus are very environmentally friendly.

How far can you drive on an electric car's charge? The amazing fact is that electric cars can usually travel for about a hundred miles before needing a charge. The batteries generally need charged overnight and there is a gauge that can tell you how much power you have left. They are perfectly fine for city driving and those who don't have to go long distances on a regular basis.

This next fact about electric cars may amaze you – I know it did me! Some people believe that an electric car can't go very fast. But the fact is that electric cars have been clocked at over one hundred miles per hour and can go from zero to that in less than nine seconds! This is because electric motors have a very high torque which allows them to accelerate quickly and travel faster.

There are many more facts to be found out about electric cars such as their price, their range, their availability, and their benefits. Finding out these facts is easy. If you are thinking about buying an electric car, do your research and find one that fits your lifestyle. Most car companies produce at least a hybrid type of electric car that runs on both gasoline and electricity, but you can also find total electric cars if you know where to look. Just get the facts and then get on the electric car bandwagon. You may just find out you like it there!

New Electric Car Batteries- Every Car Freak's Dream Battery!

Batteries are used to run electric cars, they are stored beneath the hood and maybe 12 to 24 in numbers.

When it is time to replace them they are all there.

These batteries are similar to those used on cell phones and toy cars children love to drive around in the backyard. Thus, it is not very difficult to get new batteries when we need them.

Actually, electric batteries do not need to be replaced often so replacement of batteries does not happen too frequently.

They cost around $2000 to $5000 , depending on the model and make of your car.

You must be careful about the amount of electricity in the battery before charging it.

Sometimes the batteries have an in built "memory" , and if the battery is not run completely before charging it may lose some of its potency. In this situation you may have to spend on a new battery before it is due.

There is allot of research and development underway in the electric cars industry.

New battery technology is being worked on to ensure that your vehicle can get charged faster and hold more power for a longer time. It will not be long before you can drive your car longer without the need for a battery charge. This is really some great news for those who patronize electric cars. At present the cars can run up to 100 miles per charge. There is a strong possibility that by 2010 the car will be able to run 200 miles on new batteries.

Recycling of the batteries can be done when it is time to replace the batteries.

Electric car batteries are recyclable up to 95 percent. Only those who are concerned about the environment and want to protect their wallets against the gasoline price hike will opt for an electric car, since you have, you are sure to be one of them. So, if you can recycle your electric car battery, before buying a new one you have given yourself a new source of power along with peace of mind.

It is advisable to choose the best type of batteries, for the best price, for your car and be assured that you have done the best for yourself and for the environment.

E85 Ethanol Alternative Fuel

Using E85 Ethanol as an alternative fuel has become almost a rage in the United States. There is a new trend towards making our transportation needs more environmentally friendly. As global warming is becoming a growing concern, more and more people want to do their part to make sure that we have a world to live in for the next 2,000 years. Using E85 Ethanol as an alternative fuel for your vehicle is a great way to start.

E85 Ethanol is a product that contains 85 percent ethanol and 15 percent gasoline. Ethanol is basically a grain alcohol that is made from corn, soybeans, and even plant waste and trash like paper. Besides its superior performance characteristics, ethanol burns cleaner than gasoline; it is a completely renewable, domestic, environmentally friendly fuel that enhances the nation's economy and energy independence.

Today, the U. S. imports more than half of its oil and overall consumption continues to increase. By supporting ethanol production and use, U.S. drivers can help reverse that trend. Using E85 Ethanol as an alternative fuel source can reduce pollution. Government tests have shown that E85 vehicles reduce harmful hydrocarbon and benzene emissions when compared to vehicles running on gasoline. E85 Ethanol can also reduce carbon dioxide (CO_2), a harmful greenhouse gas and a major contributor to global warming.

Although CO_2 is released during ethanol production and combustion, it is recaptured as a nutrient to the crops that are used in its production. Unlike fossil fuel combustion, this unlocks carbon that has been stored for millions of years, use of ethanol results in low increases to the carbon cycle. E85 Ethanol as an alternative fuel also degrades quickly in water and, therefore, poses much less risk to the environment than an oil or gasoline spill.

There are many vehicles on the market today that are already E85 Ethanol compatible, so you can use this as an alternative fuel to gasoline. A second option is to have your current car converted from a gasoline engine to an E85 Ethanol compatible engine. You will want to have this conversion done by a licensed mechanic, but it can be done!

Energy Conservation And Alternative Fuel

We all know that there is a trend toward using alternative fuel to help the environment, and E85 Ethanol is one of the first ones to contribute toward that trend. It is currently available in many places and can do wonders for improving your car's efficiency as well as your wallet. With the rising price of gasoline, it's really a good idea to explore E85 Ethanol as an alternative fuel source for your vehicle.

Ethanol Fuel Varieties And Vehicles That Run On Them!

Suddenly there is a lot of talk going on about alternative fuels. One can be assured that ethanol and gasoline blends of up to 10% ethanol can be used to run some vehicles . So there need not be any worries about how this combination can be used for vehicles. There are some states which need the monthly or all- year use of ethanol up to 10% as a type of oxygenate additive to tone down the formation of the ozone layer.

Remember, low percentage oxygenate will blend, like ethanol fuel is not traditionally what is alternative fuels in vehicles. Ethanol vehicles are vehicles which are made specially to run on up to 15% gasoline (E85),85% denatured ethanol or any combination of the two in which Ethanol limit is up to 85%.In colder climates E85 can be adjusted in such a way that the actual ratio of E 85 is less than 85%Ethanol. Vehicles which use E85 are also known as FFVs or flexible fuel vehicles .

Right now there are many kinds of ethanol fuels being made and it is tough to decide which kind of fuel will suit which vehicle. Light - duty FFvs comprise of a large collection of vehicles which may range from compacts to sport utility vehicles to pick up trucks.

FFvs have only one fueling system contrary to the bi-fuel natural gas as well as propane vehicles that have two exclusive fueling systems. A vehicle has to be able to use fuel blends up to 85% ethanol to be eligible to be certified as an alternative fuel vehicle (AFV)for tax credits , incentives to meet requirements for authorized fleets(federal, state, and fuel provider fleets) under the Energy Policy Act of 1992(EPAct).

In places like the Midwest where corn is grown in abundance, a large number of people use ethanol as a type of fuel for their vehicles.E85 is so popular amongst vehicle user in the Midwest that one finds long queues in the pump which sells E85.

But for us who use gasoline run vehicles it pinches our pocket when we have to pay a premium on the cheap gasoline. Anyway, with the new tendency of using fuel which burns without pollution the price of ethanol can be made lower than gasoline as supply equals demand. At present the supply of Ethanol is higher than its demand. Shortly ,this could be turned upside down and the price of all kinds of ethanol fuel could be lowered to run our vehicles.

Government Grants For Alternative Fuel

The alternative fuel industry has grown in popularity over the years, and the Federal as well as State governments are getting involved like never before. Legislation is being introduced every day offering government grants for using alternative fuels. That means that research and technology can continue to progress as it has for several years now as scientists and researchers find new ways to provide us with power other than standard fossil fuels.

What types of government grants are available when it comes to the use of alternative fuels? Well, most of them involve businesses who are interested in converting their gas-powered vehicle fleets over to alternative fuel fleets that are environmentally friendly and will meet with the Energy Policy Act that President Bush signed in 2005.

Businesses such as trucking companies use a large amount of fossil fuels. The increasing cost of gasoline makes their operating costs rise and, in turn, passed on to the consumer – that's us! When these companies begin to convert their trucks over to alternative fuel and get a government grant to pay for the cost, they're saving money, and so are we!

Of course, these government grants won't cover the cost of switching to alternative fuel sources entirely. However, many grants can amount to millions of dollars of free money with the companies only having to pay about half of what is required to convert engines.

Some people don't agree with the thought of their tax dollars paying for something like paying for companies to convert vehicles to alternative fuel vehicles. However, if they really thought about the advantages, they might actually change their mind and begin supporting the government grant program for alternative fuel use.

For example, allowing the government to provide grant money for those who want to use alternative fuels, we are decreasing our dependence on foreign oil and thus becoming much more self-sufficient. This will also help with the alarming phenomenon of global warming, which is a reality, and has been brought to the forefront through ex-Vice President Al Gore's Oscar winning documentary "An Inconvenient Truth".

Energy Conservation And Alternative Fuel

All of us in the United States should really be concerned about both of these problems: dependence on foreign oil and global warming. By getting involved with grant programs, the government is doing what it can to insure that we can find solutions to the problems instead of just sitting back and doing nothing. Alternative fuels are the wave of the future and having the support of the government through grant money can help make us a totally independent country when it comes to our energy sources.

Energy Conservation: Why It's So Important

As someone that has to pay bills each month, you already know the importance of energy conservation. There is no way for you to have not noticed that your bills have been increasing. It has happened and is one thing that you just should consider doing. But, energy conservation is not always something that is on our minds. If you find yourself only thinking about it when the bills for the month arrive, then you may be missing the boat.

Why You Need To Know

Energy conservation is helpful in a number of ways to each of us. The most profound way that affects us directly is the cost. If you just turn off a few lights, you may not notice it. But, if you do several things to keep yourself in line with your energy goals, you may find yourself able to really save money here. Energy costs continue to rise and even if they slow down in that rise, they are not likely to come down. If you want to cut your bill down, then, you must use less energy.

Yet, there are other reasons for conserving energy as well. Consider, for example, the fact that one of the most vital fuels that we all rely on is that of oil. Some scientists believe that we will run out of oil within the next 60 years. Can you image the cost of your bills then? Still, consider the fact that many of these energy needs also produce toxins in the air. That makes them not only running out but also destroying the environment while they do it.

As you can see, there are many reasons why you, as a citizen of Earth should consider energy conservation in your daily life. Even if you just cut back slightly here and there, you will notice a difference in your bill but not necessary in your overall lifestyle. There are many benefits to taking care of the energy we use. It is a good thing for all of us to take into consideration as well. The end result is a result that satisfies everyone's needs.

Find a few ways that you too can cut down on the amount of energy that you use. Challenge yourself to a few different limits. See if you can save just $5 this month on your electric bill. See if you can conserve energy for your own and for the world's well being.

Energy Conservation Tips

Energy conservation is something we all need to do to protect the earth and to protect our pocket books. If you have not considered the benefits of taking advantage of a few extra dollars, then you should start here. Remember that the small things add up but there are also some important things that you should remember as well that can help you to stop using as much energy within your home. In most cases, you will never even notice the difference in them either. That is until you get the much lower bill for them.

Tips To Get You Started

Here are a few tips to take into consideration for energy conservation. Do these things today. Incorporate your family in the process and you will save even more.

- **Your shower.** Take a shower over a bath. You will use less water in a shower then you will by taking a bath. That means less hot water usage and in turn less energy to heat the water. Bath tubs take a huge amount of water to fill up, leaving you with much more energy needs. That is unless you happen to take very long showers and in that case, try to cut down on the length of your shower for sheer improvement in your energy bills quickly.
- **Laundry.** When washing clothing, consider washing in the coldest setting allowable for the fabric. Do not over dry clothing. Set your timer to alert you as soon as the laundry is dry rather than when the timer ticks on. IN addition, only wash clothing in full loads. Smaller loads just waste water and money in energy. You may also want to consider new detergents that claim to be able to wash your laundry with just as much benefit in cold water.
- **Your cooking habits.** The way that you cook also makes a difference. In the summer, use the grill which will keep the heat from the oven out of the home. In the winter, back breads and make dinner around the middle to late afternoon when it is the coldest. This will help to keep up your home. Your cook top should also be used more often then your oven as it uses less energy to work.

You can easily add these into your every day usage and see benefits right away from doing so. Energy conservation does not have to be hard or challenging, but should be smart.

Energy Conservation: Save Gas

One of the first ways that you can learn energy conservation is through the use of gas savings. Most of us know all too well about the cost of gas today. To fuel your vehicle you are likely going to need to take on another job soon! That's what many people think and say, but the truth is that all they need to do is to learn how to conserve energy instead. With your vehicle, there are a number of small things that can easily add up to saving you gas in the long run.

Here are some tips that you can take care of today and start saving gas on right away.

- **To conserve fuel for your car, check out your tires.** If your tires are not filled correctly, you will not get the most mileage for your vehicle. If they are under or over filled, you could be wasting money. If you are not sure, check your owner's manual for specifications. Check your tires at least once per week.

- **Change your oil.** You should follow your manufacturer's directions on how often you should have your car's oil changed. Doing this regularly will allow you to get the highest function from the vehicle including in gas savings.

- **Drive correctly.** Do not step on the gas pedal hard. Ease into speed. Drive at the speed limit which has been created to help you to save gas. If you drive quickly and start quickly, the vehicle needs to use more fuel and that wastes money in your pocket.

- **Most experts agree that there is little fuel savings from more expensive qualities of fuel.** Stick to the lower costing product unless your vehicle specifies a higher quality is a must.

- **Driving with the windows up or down does not matter as much as having the air conditioning on full blast.** Even on the freeway, keeping your windows down and the air conditioning off is much more cost effective.

Energy conservation is easy to do in your vehicle. Most vehicles are improving in their gas mileage but there is still a long way to go. You may even want to consider a hybrid which burns fuel much slower and more efficiently. Can you conserve fuel in this way?

Energy Conservation: Check Your Windows

In energy conservation, one of the most important things for you to consider in your home is your windows. In fact, in some cases, upwards of 35 to 60% of your energy loss comes directly from the windows in your home. If you have poor quality windows or you do not have the right seals around them, you are simply losing money. Since windows are something you do not want to give up, there are several ways that you can learn to improve them to get the most out of them.

Tips To Improvement

- If you have very leaky or old windows, you must consider if it is time to consider replacing. Should you do so, consider Energy Star quality windows. These will save you the most money in the long run. High quality, double pane windows are necessary to keep the cold out and the heat in (or the other way around in the summer.)

- Take a candle, light it and run it along the closed windows on a windy day. When you do this, you will see the flame flicker if there is a leak in the windows and the air is getting in. If this happens, take the time to properly seal the window to prevent energy loss through this crack.

- Closely inspect both the outside and the inside of the window. If you find loose fittings, missing caulking or any broken panes, fix them as soon as possible. These are all leaking out your energy needs.

- During the winter months to prevent energy loss, consider purchasing air tight window coverings. These are inexpensive and offer an extra layer of protection in keeping the cold out and the heat in your home.

- Lock your windows they are supposed to be closed. Just that tiny little gap can provide enough energy loss to show considerably on your next heating bill.

The windows will provide you with beauty in your home if you can look out them knowing that you are not losing energy through them. Use the sunlight to heat a room on a winter day. Keep the drapes closed to keep air out. Whatever you do, invest in high quality windows and insure that they are well taken care of. This will allow you to gain the best possible results in energy conservation within your home.

Energy Conservation: Alternative Energy Sources

Energy conservation is something at the top of all of our minds. If you are looking at ways to save money on the energy that you use, why not consider some other, lesser expensive and environmentally less tasking fuel sources? If you did not think this was necessary or that they would work in your home, consider again. In fact, you may love some of these options once you are able to purchase and use them. They are sure to save you a good amount of money right away.

What's Out There?

There are several alternative energy sources, but the best ones are those that are naturally renewable. Consider these, for example.

Solar Light: Solar panels are so in demand that they are backed up in sales for years, in some locations. Solar energy comes from the sun. The panels take that sunlight (solar rays) and use them as it would any other fuel. For night time use, the panels store fuel to be used when you call on it to be used. What's more is that once you purchase the solar panels you have no real cost to using solar energy. Today, outdoor lights, school buildings and even entire grocery stores are being run on solar light.

Wind Power: Why not put to use the wind? Many locations are doing just that. By setting up large windmills, they are able to generate quite a bit of energy. In some locations, wind power powers the entire town. Wind is renewable and completely clean. Why not tap into it then?

Water Power: Take a quick look at Niagara Falls, one of the Seven Wonders of the World located in Canada. Those falls are huge and the power that they generate is massive just from falling water. The city has been running on just water power for some time. As a renewable source and clean burning fuel, you can see how this energy is one to consider as well.

All of these alternative forms of energy are options that you can and can take full advantage of. There are plenty more as well. Corn is fast becoming the source for taking over for gasoline in cars. Some cities are taking food waste or even animal waste and turning that into fuel as well. As you can see, alternative fuels are the best way to conserve energy. What's more is that they are completely safe for the environment too.

Energy Conservation: Small Things Add Up

When it comes to energy conservation, the small things can add up quickly. If you think that you can not afford to find a way to save on your energy bill, consider the various small things that you can do that will easily add up to savings across the board. With so many different things out there, there is no way that you will not benefit from them.

Little things do add up. If you didn't think that by turning off a few lights that you could save a considerable amount of money on your next energy bill, think again. Here are several tips that you can do today to start seeing improvements right away.

- **For car fuel savings, step on the gas pedal much slower.** Do not get to the street's mileage as quickly. Slow down early when approaching red lights. Ease onto the gas when the light turns green again. These things will greatly benefit your miles per gallon of gas.
- **Unplug all of your LED appliances.** If your coffee pot or other appliances in your kitchen have LED lights on them, they are taking up electricity just by being on. Unplug your appliances after use.
- **Check for leaks of air coming through from the electrical outlets in your home.** If you feel a draft coming in, this could be why. To conserve energy here, make sure you caulk and insulate the area.
- **Turn off the lights.** You will save a good deal of money just by turning off extra lights in your home. Open the drapes and allow the sunlight to be used instead. You will save a good deal of money by turning off just a handful of lights each day or week.
- **Use your ceiling fan instead of using your air conditioning.** Moving air just feels better and it will also help you to actually cool down without the cost of air conditioning.

Energy conservation starts with little things. Make a plan of it. Play a game and see just how many different lights the kids can keep off. There are many small things that you can do in your home, outside of your home and in your vehicle to save on energy costs. Doing so will improve your bill but also will improve the environment as well.

Energy Conservation: Conserve By Using Your Thermostat

If you plan to save some money this winter on your energy bills, consider the thermostat. This little functioning tool in your home actually plays a large role in keeping your home running smoothly. Rather, it keeps your home actually the right temperature for your day to day life. If you do not think much of it, you are probably not getting all that you can for it. If yours is old, it is time to look for an updated one that will offer many benefits to you.

What's The Thermostat's Benefit?

A thermostat controls the furnace as well as the air conditioning units within your home. You tell it what level you would like the home to be at and it will insure that it remains as close to that number as possible. The problem is that it is easy to set it and forget it. If you do not have a programmable thermostat now is the time to invest in one. They are only slightly more than a standard version and will do much more for you including saving you a considerable amount of energy.

First, consider what you have it set at. If you would like to start saving energy, experts recommend setting the thermostat at 72 F degrees during the summer months and at 68 F degrees in the winter. For every two degrees that you can comfortably lower this, you will save a good deal of money on your energy bills. Another tidbit of help; if you feel comfortable in shorts in the winter and are craving pants in the summer, your settings are off. Raising them just slightly and throwing a blanket on your bed will help you to save money.

Next, consider programming benefits that are offered with it. For example, if you work all day, why should your thermostat be keeping the house nice and toasty? You can program them to turn the furnace back up to your preferred level just an hour or so before you come home. This does not effect the way that you live your day, but it will effect that energy bill.

By doing all of these things it will help to benefit you in the long run. To keep your energy bills manageable, invest some time in programming your thermostat and using it regularly. You will find this to be one of the best tools that you have for improving your energy usage.

Energy Conservation: Consider Your Lighting

When it comes to energy conservation, lighting is something you should be taking into consideration. There is no doubt that we all need the right amount of light to function within our day. We need to see to read and simply function in each task we take on. But, what type of lighting, what amount of lighting and how that lighting is generated makes a good amount of difference in the way of energy conservation. If you have not thought about this aspect of saving energy, you are not alone.

Conserving Energy With Your Lights

The best possible light for you to use within your home to conserve lights is that of the sun. Anytime that you can get the sun into the windows to light up your home, the better off that you are. The sun is free and it can also work to heat up your home during the winter as well. If you have heavy drapes on your windows, consider removing or moving them so that you can easily allow the sun to flow in and therefore you can keep the lights off within the home.

When the sun is not cooperating with your needs, there are other things to consider as well. Energy conservation in the way of the type of lighting you use is your next big consideration. If you invest in Energy Star quality bulbs you will spend a little more to purchase them but they will outlast most other bulbs. In addition, they use a considerably less amount of energy to turn on and to run. That means that they are going to provide just as much light but without nearly as much power and for a much longer period of time. Consider fluorescent light bulbs as a main source of power for your home.

It goes without saying that you can also save on your energy bills by just turning off the lights when you are not in a room and keeping their usage to a minimum. To save even more, consider using solar powered lighting fixtures outdoors instead of electric versions. This is yet another way that you can save with lighting. Invest a bit of time in finding the right lighting sources for your home as you do not have to live in the dark. Then, use them correctly and reap the energy conserving that you will be doing.

Energy Conservation In Decorating Your Home

Did you know that you can save energy by decorating and designing your landscaping correctly? Most of us do not think about how easy it can be for us to use less energy. Although it may not be something that is on our minds, it really should be. If you plan to invest in decorating aspects of your home, consider how you can do it better to allow for more energy benefits.

What Should You Do?

Not sure where decorating comes into play with energy conservation? To help you to full understand, get started with these tips.

1. **Determine how to improve your windows.** If you use heavy draping during the winter months, you are adding an extra layer of protection to keep the heat in and the cold out. Even if you do not want to put on several layers of drapes, just keeping the blinds closed on the windows will provide a great bit of help. You can feel this energy conservation.

2. **During the summer months, consider those drapes again.** Let the light stream in and pull drapes to the side to allow for cool breezes to come in. Going without the air conditioning will conserve energy greatly, but to make that happen, you still need to allow air flow through the home. Doing this allows you to turn off more of the lights in your home too.

3. **Plant a few trees.** If you have three trees strategically placed around your home, you can lower your energy costs by some 20%. All that it takes is just the shade protection. During the summer, this shade can lower the temperature of the area by 1 to 5 degrees. In the winter, the trees act as a wind breaker keeping the blistering cold air from hitting the home. They also allow for sunlight to come through during the winter months as well.

Decorating your home in the right away can offer you many beneficial savings in energy. Just the way that your home faces can provide more or less sunlight for your needs. Think about how you can improve the energy efficiency through decorating in the right way. You may be surprised at just how beneficial some of these things can be to your home just about instantly.

Energy Conservation And The Fireplace

Is the fireplace a good thing for energy conservation or is it a potential pitfall? There is no doubt that if you have a fireplace and use it, it can be beneficial to your energy bills. If you have one and do not use it, it can be a leading cause of escaped energy within your home. Where does your home stand and what can you do to improve these things? Consider your true usage of the fireplace and your ability to benefit from it.

Things To Think About

The first thing to take into consideration is how much you actually use the fireplace. If you honestly do not use the fireplace all that often, then consider having it permanently closed. This will keep a tremendous amount of energy from escaping from your chimney during the winter and the summer months when the air conditioning and the heat are on full blast. If you do make this happen, make sure that you do not light the fireplace at all as the smoke will have no place to go.

If you do use your fireplace have it checked carefully. Make sure it has a flue in place and that it is able to keep air from coming into the home. Also, have it cleaned. A clean fireplace is one that is safe for your use. To make the most of the heat that a fire can produce, you may want to consider a heater blower which will blow the heat from the fire out into the home. This can significantly increase the amount of energy that you actually get from the fireplace.

To make this worthwhile, you do need to have a good amount of wood on hand that has been seasoned and is ready to go. Although you may not like the work of hauling wood into and out of the home, running the fireplace for just several hours a day can considerably bring down the high cost of heat during the winter months.

When used properly, the fireplace is an ideal tool for energy conservation. If you are looking for a way to save on energy, this may be a good way to do it. Yet, you must take care of a fireplace or you will burn wood too quickly and ineffectively for it to really benefit you. On a cold winter night, this is just the place to be.

This Product Is Brought To You By

www.ingramcontent.com/pod-product-compliance
Lightning Source LLC
LaVergne TN
LVHW012128070526
838202LV00056B/5909